MODERN OCEAN

Modern
Ocean

James Harms

Carnegie Mellon University Press
Pittsburgh 1992

Acknowledgments

The author would like to thank the editors of the following magazines, where these poems first appeared, sometimes in different form:

The American Poetry Review: "The Hole in the Moon"
Carolina Quarterly: "Somewhere Someone is Saying Goodbye"
Crazyhorse: "The Sequel," "My Androgynous Years"
Denver Quarterly: "Between Lives We Write the History"
Indiana Review: "Fragile Bridges," "Inherit the Earth," "Versions of Transport"
Ironwood: "'Grace to Be Born and Live,'" "Poem"
The Journal: "Fond Promise," "Y-Turn," "Days before Grace"
The Kenyon Review: "Explaining the Evening News to Corbyn," "Serious Affection," "'When You Wish upon a Star that Turns into a Plane'"
The Missouri Review: "Everywhere at Once," "Safer Shadow"
Orange Coast Review: "Fear of Angels," "Peter Case"
Ploughshares: "See How We Are"
Poetry: "Mexican Christmas," "Penance"
Poetry East: "Homecoming," "Stories"
The Southern Poetry Review: "Breakfast on the Patio"
Three Rivers Poetry Journal: "Isabelle's Sister," "So Long Lonely Avenue"

The poems "Peter Case" and "'When You Wish upon a Star that Turns into a Plane'" also appeared in *Sweet Nothings: An Anthology of Rock and Roll in American Poetry,* from Spoon River Press.

The poems "Between Lives We Write the History" and "Reasons to Live" appeared as separate broadsides from Westcott Press of Altadena, California. Thanks to Jeff Carpenter.

The author would like to thank Yaddo and the MacDowell Colony for fellowships that aided the writing of this book, and Denison University for its generous support.

Special thanks to the following for their help and friendship: Peter Cameron, Lynda Hull, Aleda Shirley, Dean Young and, especially, Ralph Angel and David Wojahn.

Publication of this book is supported by grants from the National Endowment for the Arts in Washington, D.C., a Federal agency, and from the Pennsylvania Council on the Arts.

Library of Congress Catalog Card Number: 91-72058
ISBN 0-88748-126-4
ISBN 0-88748-127-2 Pbk.
Copyright © 1992 by James Harms
Printed and bound in the United States of America

Contents

for my family
and with thanks to Lani

Charlotte once ran away from me, outside the studio,
and I grabbed her dress to stop her, to keep her near me.
A yellow cotton dress I loved because it was too long for
her. I still have a lemon-yellow mark on the palm of my
right hand. Oh, God, if I'm anything by a clinical name,
I'm a kind of paranoiac in reverse. I suspect people of
plotting to make me happy.

—J.D. Salinger
("Raise High the Roof Beam, Carpenters")

Mexican Christmas

We drove all night to the border
and across, through Tijuana and Rosarito,
pulled into Cantamar as the chickens
walked out to Christmas morning.
Your friend Alberto opened his market
to sell us cases of *Bohemia*

and we sat with his wife on the porch
admiring the new hotel
careening off the beach.
She gave us two pounds of yesterday's
tortillas in a wet towel
then sent us off down the road

to La Mision. We are back again this year,
a day later; Christmas is behind us.
Below us Toby has written a message
in the sand and turns to wave.
You smile at the giant letters
and slowly tee-up a golf ball

on the patio. Toby begins to run
and you crack a five iron
and point at the horizon,
where brown pelicans dip low
in the troughs of today's best set.
And later we walk up to La Fonda

to sit in a line at the pink tile bar,
six of us facing the ocean.
I listen to you try to talk to a woman
from Diamond Bar whose husband sleeps
at a table by the window.
You ask her easy questions

and lean into her,
blow her cigarette smoke back
through her lips. She says
it's just not her day
to listen to someone like you.
I stare at her and want to light

her next cigarette. I want to tell her
how important you are to everyone
who's ever known you;
but she explains it to me.
"Your friend," she says.
"When he looked at me that way,

it made me wish I was him."
She turns back to her ice cubes.
I think she's comfortable looking at them
when the only person
she's certain of at this moment
can't lift his head off the table.

Penance

I was twelve when my father saved
a thousand Blue Chip stamps and traded
them for rods and reels. On weekends

he loaded them in the car while I
made sandwiches and my brother rolled towels
into perfect tubes. We'd drive south

to Lake Ryan to fish, and I never wondered
if the act was sacred, never noticed
each blue gill was weighed against his watch.

One afternoon, my brother took control
of the small rented outboard; he was ten
and ready my father said. Clouds hovered

in the distance and Tom steered in close
to shore, as if evading the bad weather.
I watched my father: he seemed afraid

I decided, so far from his new wife
and the life they were starting over,
though the sky already was clearing

and the rain at the lake's far end
would never reach us. Tom cut the engine
late and brought the boat in hard

against the dock, his blue eyes feigning
surprise and fooling my father, who paid
the attendant five extra dollars to stop

yelling. Tom remembers the man's gray cheeks,
his two flat palms reaching out to check
the speeding boat. I see my father's

eyes on the ride home, rising again
and again to the rear view mirror.
As if the lights pulling close and passing

carried the secret he'd left out on the lake,
his two boys ignoring their cheap tackle
and fishing anyway. He wasn't sure

if ever they'd know a moment of profound
overwhelming persuasion, or if this road
beyond his exit did, in fact, go on forever.

The Book of My Forgetting

Yesterday's a distance
I'm feeling better about, almost
close enough to listen to.

Like the evening sliding down around me,
even sturdier than I'd hoped,
foothills slipping in the rusty light
and Sarah in the garden
solving problems with a trowel.

Over the years the song bumps
to a stop less conveniently,
just when you're beginning to feel okay,
almost dancing. Even then
the quiet has momentum, like night falling
or a long drink of hose water still
warm from the afternoon.

And though there's hope in the empty glass
you hold thoughtfully in your hand,
somewhere a lung completes the slow turn
to black, a voice gives over its vehicle,
and you begin to shrug
uncontrollably. These days seem important,

it seems you should hold them
responsible for your worry, the floating
balance and broken promise.
But the book of regrets, lying open
beside your hand, isn't doing you
any good, though it's lovely
as blue paint on a length of silk,
how words arrange themselves

if left alone. How possibility
is a confusion of willingness and fear—
fear you've got it wrong again,
that your vision of sitting quietly
and doing nothing is a symptom of pressure
at the back of your skull. But you go on.
You have to.

Sarah ties a knot in her shirt front
and runs a hand through her hair.
From here the smudge of dirt on her forehead
could be the start of her vanishing.
So much so I walk outside to put my hand
in her pocket, and feel the air fill with what
we feel for each other, a less visible evening.

My Androgynous Years

I had a crisis at the supermarket, yesterday.
I said to myself softly, so no one could hear,
I said, Your soul is *not* stepping
from your body. I said, Stop it, relax.
And I did. I held it all together
past the magazines and gum,
through 8-Items-or-Less and out the door.
I sat in my car and let mascara
run down my arms like greasy rain.
Until a woman in a Volvo beeped
and pointed at the asphalt under me,
unwilling, I guess, to wait any longer.
When I was eight my sister hated me.
She hated clothes and make-up.
She hated buckled shoes.
We'd walk Vermillion Street beneath
the insect sizzle of neon
to buy my mother cigarettes,
loiter like felons till
all seemed clear in Lee's Liquor-Mart.
I'd ask Peter Lee where the Cokes had gone
and he'd come around to help me look
while my sister snaked her hand to a packet
of Pall Malls and was gone. On the way home,
sometimes, she ran ahead, easy over long legs.
She'd find a crumbling vestibule
to soothe her shadow down to stone,
and time my slow arrival.
We'd sit near a puddle of ragwater
or piss, her laughter a hand against
my neck, and wait for my sobs to soften.
I share my lunch today with a boy from
Peru, Indiana. He recites King's
"I Have a Dream" speech
rising off the bench to shake his fists

at the assembled phantoms.
Pigeons scatter and regather, and all around us
haloes appear and vanish, the fountain mist
blown in rainbows and to pieces.
He is splendid and I offer all my Fritoes.
One night he will come to me like a dream
on the television, and announce
a special offer: laser-sharpened knives
or a three-record set.
But that's the future. For now
we hold hands and talk about the news,
which is much better than yesterday's
but only half as good as tomorrow's.

Y-Turn

"A change is better than a rest"
     —Elvis Costello

I'm pretty sure last week you thought of me.

There was this man who worked where I did,
and in those ways of sliding through the day's events
without involvement, we knew each other.
At coffee one day he told me
the fence beside his house had fallen down,
and his lunatic neighbor with all the cats
just hung around staring. I nodded and said
I knew how that went. He asked for a cigarette.

Sometimes I'd watch him at the office
waiting for elevators or standing there
xeroxing reports or whatever. He never seemed
lonely or incomplete, though maybe with drinks after work
he'd try too hard. I think he just wanted to be okay.
But a woman down the street saw his lawn begin to weed;
she was nice enough to care and not say anything.
A man sets off for work, does a Y-Turn
in your driveway, and you nod while
hosing the zinnias or wave a little. But anyway,
one day she never saw him again; or rather, she realized
she hadn't seen him, or something. So she phoned.

And I thought he'd just had enough, that somehow, somewhere
he was making a go of it. A fresh start.
Then I bumped into him downtown, so we went for coffee.
He told me the house was never his,
that his mother left it on condition it never be sold,
and how could you own something you couldn't sell.
The fence fell down and, well, things led to things.

He took a cigarette and thanked me,
shook his head and pulled a slip of paper from somewhere,
slid it across to me. I remember how worried I was about it,
all the little puddles of coffee and milk on the table.
It went, "A change is better than a rest," and I said
I didn't get it. It's a song he said,
and he sang that one line as if it wasn't even us
sitting in the middle of a coffee shop.

Then he went back to smoking, turned his face away and
issued a quiet cloudy whistle. I hadn't thought of you
in months, but that second I did. And you know how
sometimes you just know the object of your thoughts
is thinking of you too?

for Bob Tafoya

Reasons to Live

We wake too early, and wonder,
and think to call someone,
though maybe it isn't worth
talking about, how the gentler needs
remain intact long after
the wedding, the first child.
So we work up our nerve and worry.

And a woman has recently
given up, inflates
a pair of waterwings
while her son sticks his toe
in the pool and leans back amazed,
the one cloud like a hammer
at the start of its fall.
The gardener kicks through a bank of daisies
on his way to a muddy pickup.
And out of sight for the time being
a girl in a white dress is dreaming
of eyes the color of autumn.
She stands at her mother's window
singing hymns to calm herself.

*

We have in common the beginning and the end,
though who really thinks of them
in the blaze of gardens and blue pools,
the slow dance, the sad embrace.

I wish we'd been children together.
As if the years before knowing
were rehearsals for a play
we've no obligation to perform.

And we haven't, have we?
Ash fills the pool. The cats
grow up and ignore us.
And the neighbor says his wife
doesn't like your new tree, how it
wrecks the sunlight through her windows.
You nod and he nods. That's how it is,
things try to run away with our lives.

Until, backed up to the people we love,
we turn and find ourselves in school yards
on Christmas Eve, replaying a perfect wedding
before a gathering of friends. Friends convinced
we are exactly who we should be.

for Cody

Homecoming

to Tom

Somewhere music rounds a corner
and begins its way toward us.

You are trying to steer me home
through the moonlight, to hold me

in this stationary heaven—
trying to quiet my clumsy stumble,

the vowels I can't round into anything
sensible in these alleys

close to home. Around us
ground fog rises, erasing our shoes

and folded cuffs, and the neon
statements of this familiar street blur

and turn to apparitions
of speechlessness. When our father

made this walk, or drove it,
dangerous, in the grey Plymouth,

we sat awake in our room above
the garage, listening for

his voice or a door slamming,
anything. And as darkness settles now

I kneel at the curb and grip
my knees, overwhelmed by a separate

loneliness, even as you whisper
It will be alright, and rest

a hand on my shoulder.
I know that you love me,

that we loved our father.
But there is nothing I can do about it.

Fond Promise

In a certain light there's nothing to lose.
Say the porch light I return to
at 15, cold from a night
of straightening Christmas trees
in the supermarket parking lot,
hammering in the cross plank stands
and pulling them loose again.
And Mrs. Bergland, whose son can't be left
alone or find an answer in feeding himself,
or even walk too close to anything,
his anxious fingers clumsy and dull—
Mrs. Bergland picks a smallish fir
and helps her boy tie it down in the trunk.
Or out behind the rectory my sister
lights a match and sets a model airplane
on a stump to burn. From my room above
the garage I see a bloom of flame curl
around the plastic, my Messerschmidt,
its silver prop turning in the heat,
rubber wheels melting.
And I know she is breathing the fumes,
will spin away across the yard
like loose paper pinwheeling in the wind.
I watch a long time
because I can't look away:
the small fire; the ragged orange trees.
My sister, frail as smoke
in the shift and tear of sunlight.

Dogtown

Venice, California

Funny how the kid you always punched
remembers you fondly.
Standing at the taco stand
exchanging numbers, laughing,
he keeps looking around, keeps
shrugging for no good reason.
He says, "Do you remember when..."
then leaves mid-sentence
to answer a ringing payphone.

Around you it's Sunday.
A tattooed fat man sells postcards
of himself. The Spanish shawl
glides by on her Schwinn.
A little boy kneels to strap his sandal,
the ocean a blue terrace behind him.

Some days, when the smog
blows inland at dusk,
you stare out where Japan should be
and count backward the people who love you.
The sun sprays kites across the water,
a V of pelicans drops softly behind the waves.
You see islands in the channel, a boat
or two coming home from sea.
Evelyn, your neighbor, walks her parrot

every evening, first down the strand
then to O'Pepe's for a beer.
When she sees you she stops, squats down
beside her bird.
She lifts his beak until he's looking,
and she points, says your name.
Some days, she says it three or four times.

"Grace to Be Born and Live"

in memory of Frank O'Hara

The moo tonight and all that other nonsense
snag in ch > trees. There's a lot of noise
about activism and the new age—
to ignore it and sit with suede meatloaf
in ROSE'S would water my drying cells.
I am already shimmering like a foal.
If I called you, you would tease
about the nearness of my ideas to yesterday's rain,
dried already to smog-dust
on my old blue car. You would tease about
my old blue car too, though it brought me
all the way from Kentucky.
I drive it to RAJI'S, and a leopard
paces the cage in my heart.
Shall I call you from here, in Hollywood?
Thelonious Monster has laid aside their instruments
and talk with towering hair to the audience.
Someone has asked about tuning a guitar with dirt
and now a bottle is chasing words through the air.
I know a lounge on Melrose where
two men in strapless gowns and tiaras sing along
with dire sensitivity to a jukebox of Ella Fitzgerald singles.
There is a window of Hockneys on Wilshire Boulevard
including one in the semi-Egyptian style.
Further along is the Carnation Building
with its overwhelming pink flower nestled in the C.
So much to see so quickly, is one way to say it,
though I would prefer a fast drive north
from Will Rogers Beach, the speed of seeing
more cinematic from the windows of an old blue car.
A strange fear has found me and it goes like this:
the stolen hour returns with everything
I would have done, and none of it is remotely kind.
I consider this an illness, to be reminded of every

injury delivered or intended. Oh well, forget it.
I am a few feet from the latest limousine
to drag its belly to Sunset Boulevard
and thinking if I'd known you, if I'd dropped from
my mother an epoch earlier (though she wouldn't be
my mother), I might not have been nice to you.
I guess that's silly.
Inside the limousine a woman beats out the time
of her private song on the chauffeur's headrest.
Her companion is asleep.
You've arrived, I want to yell,
but there are others around, and they are laughing.
If I lived in Century City I would be nearly home now.
The wrack of this evening washes by the curb.
Her name is Lois and she says she knew you.

"When You Wish upon a Star that Turns into a Plane"

—The Replacements

My clothes are standing up without me,
though it's just the bus is here,
the noise of people pulling things
into line. And I don't want a ride
but the driver leans out the door
as if to pull me into heaven.

So I light a french fries wrapper
and think: Go away, and he does.
The door folds shut and, woosh,
there goes the bus.

A bum sits down next to me and cups
a cigarette that isn't there—
he shakes his hand and takes a drag.
The air is brown around us, like an old
snapshot; I spend three minutes
trying not to breathe, just sipping a little,
then walk up to Sunset Boulevard
where on good days with God willing
I can hitchhike all the way to the beach.
I am sure that the sea will rise one day
and drive its way inland, but not today.
Today will end with a colorful dusk,
a stain the length of California
fading as the sun goes down.

When I was small there was always a meal
that everyone agreed on, and the stars
falling over the city.
I'd watch the ocean from my parents' roof
and Catalina on some days, like a cupped
hand above the smog. It's fourteen miles and three

transfers from here to Pasadena,
and my mother has said on the phone
that she loves me regardless of what
I'm taking. What am I taking?

I remember who I am and where I'm from
and I don't remember why.
But this is nothing to cry about,
so I don't. I sit down
and wave past another bus.
I watch myself flicker in its windows.

Serious Affection

Are you okay, she asks
from wherever she is.
A storm settles on the wires between us.
She is at the bottom of the ocean
or in a phone booth. She is
waving at someone as she speaks,
or she has never been so alone.

I've moved the dust
from one corner to another.
Water boils on the stove.
I will drop a bag
of vegetables in it soon
and slice cheese for a sandwich.
There are two cans of beer in the fridge.

I've made my window into an altar:
four scented candles, incense
and a Cherokee crystal.
A pine tree is buried to its waist
in the yard.
Its branches brush the screen.

In the street below, a boy
calls his sister home for dinner.
Her name is Mary, each
syllable a separate breeze
through pine needles and candle smoke.
The phone is sticky
and feels like food in my hand.
Like a fresh loaf of bread.
Are you okay? she asks.

I was twelve when my mother
told me where father had gone

and when he'd back: Utah, and never.
She moved the bangs off my forehead
and spoke to my collar—
We'll be fine, she said,
and she fastened the top button.
Her eyes were twin coins in a wishing pool,
and when they finally looked at me
I couldn't do anything.
I hadn't learned yet to surround
pain with my arms and smother it.

And I haven't learned yet to pass my hands
though the ghosts people leave behind
when they've taken everything else and gone.
And soon the phone I'm holding
will say Goodbye,
that it loves me, and to take care.
It will say there are
worse things than finding out before
it's too late
that you're in love with the wrong person.

The ficus is glowing in its plastic pot.
I can see an afternoon moon in the window,
a few rooftops and a spinning weather vane.
Are you okay, she asks again.

I say I'm all right,
and would she hold on for a second.
I turn the burner off
and pour the boiling water on the plant.
Outside the sky is bone-colored
and empty: the sun is setting,
the day's shape losing ground to shadows.
I shut the window on Mary's name,
on a voice that's given up
and is ready to eat alone.
Then I sit on the floor beside the phone

and wait for my hands to do something.
A small voice says my name from far away.
Then again. I answer to the air:
I'm fine. I tell the air firmly:
I'm okay.

So Long Lonely Avenue

"In this case I think
it's better to face it—
    we belong together."

—Rickie Lee Jones

I remember Lani floating from her body
and asking me to ask the surgeon for her teeth.
And how she sang over and over
"We belong together," while I carried her
to the car and folded her in, slipped a prescription
in her blouse and put her hand there, as if
pledging her allegiance, or holding her heart in.
We drove across Bloomington,
the spring air thick as a thousand feet of water.
Lani sang in her seat at a stop light as a boy
in a blue Chevy watched and frowned,
his idle erasing her song. Her head
lolled back like a child's beneath a night sky—
stars for the begging, the moon
dripping into a pail of old rainwater.
She kept singing, "We belong together."
I carried her up the stairs to bed and brought her
soup and straws to sip it through,
I brushed her hair one hundred times.
A week later, with cheeks like Dizzy Gillespie
and codeine in her veins,
Lani searched all day for cilantro
and made salsa in the middle of Indiana.
We trimmed our three rooms
with white, red and green, and invited everyone
we sort of liked to our place
for Cinco de Mayo. It was a night where
people fell down a great deal.
All year we'd looked for that apartment,
where she could work and I could work
and we could throw parties and be better forever.

But that was a small, wound-up idea
of how two people come into each other's arms
repeatedly for the time it takes to
ask for everything, and to take what's given.
Then, one day, he asks for something
she doesn't have, something she's never had,
and he asks because he knows this, that
she can't give anymore. So he leaves.

See How We Are

When I first arrived in this city I heard
coins falling through the air like rain,
light collecting on dusty sleeves,
in gum boxes and tins;
the addicts walked by a smoking pail
humming into their hands.
We hiked one afternoon
along the river, picnicked in the ruins
of a boat house and tossed sticks
in the water for Herbie,
called him back
as darkness drifted toward us like smoke
from the opposite shore.
Herbie leaned against a palm tree
and ran his paws in place,
trying to bark but just coughing.
Doves rose anyway
into the after-blue of evening,
and you whispered, *Cerulean,* pointing
at the sky, though around us there was no one.
Well, I am afraid too.
I take my face sometimes and point it
at your picture, taped with several postcards
to a mirror, one of bones in a desert
reaching for a cup of water, one from Yale.
I wish you were with me like a coin.
One night the moon rose to the height of buildings
and was as real, at least, as a window.
A man took my arm to steady himself,
each step the vertical earth.
His face had slid around his neck
and he whispered, "Thank you, love, there,"
pressed his hands to the air, veered away.
Some days I take my face and point it at your picture,
I say, I love you, I give up. It helps.

God knows where you are,
which is why I pray beneath
the Walk and the Don't Walk, my finger
on the button, or scream back at the drunks
in their own voices, butchering the gin dialect,
the ya-hoo of surrender.
But I am right here this second,
like a weed in the sidewalk. Like a weed.

The Sequel

At the public library on Sunset Boulevard
you were in love with the truth of a young girl,
though not with the young girl.
It would be illegal to love her.
You were warm as the tip of breath leading
to a promise, the philodendron growing like a cheer
beside the noisy ferns.
But when was this version of hello
nearly heartfelt? a handshake in the alcove
leading to gunshots? hands signing
the letter C like perfect broken bowls
collecting the particles per thousand?
You want the small pressure
like a fortune in your pocket,
though what's ever smart, at last, about
the standards of deliverance?
An accident tangles traffic late
on a Thursday morning, and you feel
the blanket pull across your face before
seeing the twisted motorcycle, the helmet
strapped like something cherished to the seat.
Why aren't you in that Subaru? wearing a suit?
at home with a child who looks like you?
And why stare ahead over the tops of
a thousand cars when what you want
is to face death like an argument
you really feel something about?
There's a league at least of dirty air
between you and God, but that's not it,
that's not what led you away from the cereal bowl
and an orange, the day as straight and remembered
as a line of royal palms.
You were asking Rachel about the movies,
you'd met Rachel at Benson's in Newport the night
before. She'd seen the sequel to a movie

you'd never heard of, and it was Damn good, she said.
Better than the first one.
You were in the public library on Sunset last Sunday
and you remembered your friend, one of Rilke's
children, the scarves he seemed to pull
from some forgotten sleeve, how he hated saying good-bye.
And then the young girl said, We're about
to close, and you looked at her as if she could
change your life. She couldn't. She almost said it.
She almost said, I cannot do a thing for you. She said,
You'll have to leave now.

Everywhere at Once

Driving in rain
on South Laguna's backstreets,
thinking I saw you by the road
and trying to stop to get it down
on a gas receipt, what you

looked like this time,
I nearly had you back.
But as quickly
that chance passed and it was
just me again, wanting

to be someone's, lining up
my favorite records and spending
the day with them. So it doesn't
surprise me, yesterday's walk
down streets of shop windows,

none of which offered up your
reflection at my side
or the shallowest gift I might
rush in to buy for you.
We strolled on, watching

the Thrift & Loan's walls
shift from blue to silver,
our faces visibly changed
in the turning light.
With everyone else I craned

and stared at the threatening
cloud, forgetting for a moment
your slim bearing in this
sudden shade. You were gone.
And I swear I'd hold a flame

in my throat to have you again
pull me into your arms.
We would share the comfort
of some familiar high. Maybe
watch the ficus ruminate

its pot of earth. Later we'd walk
to Victoria Beach—do you remember
the pier where once you laid
your coat on my shoulders
like a pitiful hug?

And I took it not thinking
of how slack the sleeves
would feel against my sides,
not thinking it today
but remembering their movement

in the wind, our wandering out there
above the sea, where just now
I thought of you.

Safer Shadow

So far we believe something
happened yesterday.
There is evidence in a friend's
reluctance to talk.
And I know you've sewn your pockets shut,
that there's smoke where your
heart used to be.
But we've got to let go of all that,
of what we like about each other,
or risk becoming photographs
of bad judgment.
Before we know it the air
is blue and slippery,
evening vanishes up a sleeve.
The pill I take reminds me of you,
which is a lot like being you.
Yesterday I collected the pictures of us
and wrote "Why?" in the borders.
It's as if we never happened.
As if we never sat around
wondering what to do.
And then doing it.
There's a fold of moonlight
by the window, an envelope
beneath the door,
but neither holds instructions for
sitting quietly in the arms of a shadow.
And I've decided to be a holder of hands,
though it wasn't my first choice.
They were all out of the gloves you wear.

Fragile Bridges

If I knew what to ask
you'd mistake this prayer for paying attention.
For what's faith but good timing
and generosity? And, sadly,
we no longer each wear shoes the other
stoops to see.
Here are the things I never said.
That two kites and a cloud make the sky
look expensive. And there is no way of telling
bell metal from shells
when the church is in ruins.
Frozen to the fence, a bird is remembering summer
and singing.
I, too, have my obligations.
I turn from them, from this window.

*

You touched the skin
beneath my eye before the lights came up,
before whatever made us cry
was smeared senseless
as a penny left resting
on the track.
The streets that winter night bore the speed
of a century unspooling, beggars
chanting through flames,
the separate skills of hope
and endurance wound tight
as a wick.
But there were ways of moving
in the darkness,
faded signs and fragile bridges,
ways of finding ourselves home.

*

I spend the morning loading the blue trunk
to send ahead, wrapping shirts
in paper and remembering them as gifts,
as advice you gave me over the slow years.
Lately I'm less worried about loneliness;
and the regrets I've lived with for so long
fold neatly and vanish
like towels of morning fog.
We'll never be ourselves again,
which makes us kinder somehow, though
not as pleased beneath umbrellas, as fast
across wet grass,
and nearly everything now wears a negligee of sadness.
There is nothing I can do to change
the easy quiet, and there are no cures for memory.
But when we're older, and bruised through,
we'll look back on all this, our years together,
and we'll cry.

Moods for Moderns

Toward the end of our childhood
your knees begin to mend,
and the awkward angle
of trees to earth
softened in your eyes like faces
above a candle. And now,

with light falling toward a morning moon
and men walking the river, we'll
be delivered to evening intact and invisible,
gathering patience with each
sweepstakes, each nickel in the can.

How strange
to change the names of streets.
How strange to be with you
without a home,
ashamed to admit we've missed another Christmas,

the sky racing away like a dizzy, deep kiss.
Not even the stars in their slots
can lead us back,
though we'll wait willingly for evening,
wishing the man squashing cans would look at us

and walk over, touch our chests
and say: "You used to live here, and you."
And we did. We did. Time was

we'd gather bottles in paper sacks
and trade glass for wine,
promise comfort like fidelity
and to hold each other
through the reckoning.

And though eternity remains aloof
we're never an arm's length apart.
As if erasure and silence
are the certainties of solitude.
As if the end is as
near as letting go.

You said once you'd never bruise
and I believed you. You said once
we'd live forever, light falling
like old bandages in the town
we used to live in.

Poem

Firemen wax their trucks
in the soft daylight of a February Sunday,
the air thin as a tissue
and warm at the edges.
Their hands swim
across sideboards and one whistles
unrecognizably a recent hit,
while a boy shakes loose his last drops
beside a palm tree
and looks back at me, and walks away pleased.
I have been more alive than this, but not much.
Where did the gulls go in Palma
when dry fountains filled with dust
or with evening, and the copper light
drifted like a fragrance through the streets?
Orange blossoms and brandy lifted
into the breeze, and it was not heaven
but it was just like heaven,
it was in that neighborhood.
I left a room down the block
paid for and empty, a glass of beer
by an ashtray, and I was
holding hands with the air.
A man piled branches in a cart
and began to tug toward an alley.
And repeatedly his wheels stuck, mudfrozen
or old, until I rose and turned my chair
to face the empty restaurant,
the bored waiter by the bar
reading a menu.
I wanted a language I could learn
but never would, a confined gesture
like fingers in a beard
or arms folding and refolding.
We floated lemons in bowls of wine

and fed each other almonds and pale asparagus.
Until the bruise of shallow talk
pushed us out into the streets,
where, separate, we found tables
of irrevocable silence. I have kept mine.
And when spring ends and the tourists reappear
I will return to us where we wait,
talking to each other and to passersby
or to our hands,
stunning to opacity the air
until it is unbreathable.

Inherit the Earth

We've arrived at the house where
friends once built small blazes that offered a way
through the woods. But there's no one home,
the curtains are different. And each window
is filled with a photograph of someone
we've known and lost track of.

Like the book once loved fallen open
to a favorite page, it's about time
we faced this, this betrayal of gifts,
bells sewn to the cuffs of children
intent on losing themselves.
The ships we trusted with precious cargoes
have leaked away the last drops;
the beaches are an unforgivable beauty.
And we're left with
the door slamming shut as we begin to understand
our lives and how to save them.
So many days begin this way, with bathwater
and few angels, a marriage in the balance.
In fact your life was comfortable
even before you grew wise enough to hate it.
But then the first indiscretion lifted free
like a cup from a speeding car,
and no explanation ended the noise of the dust
touching back to the earth. A few
stood around speechless, arms open to
the falling sun. *I remember,* said the ancient
shoe shine man, and there followed the inevitable story,
as perfect as the blind girl's touch.
We've been in this life so long it's starting to hum us
in public. How we stand on corners unable to remember
the way. How the earth sloughs off the regulars as they
mumble toward doorways, and I reach for your hand.
How I miss it and never notice, my palm filled
with the weight of sunlight and smoke.

Between Lives We Write the History

The slow rattle of blinds insists
I rise and feel my way
to the window above the parking lot.
And though it is early there are lights
dotting the neighborhood,
shapes behind windows: slow gestures
of insomniacs and the lonely.
The noise of a city just getting to its feet
is white and helpless, and I can never get back
to sleep. But this is how days begin
when they begin slowly, when the small responsibilities
filter in like a neighbor's hissing shaver.
And this is the only time I think of you,
though that isn't true. But today,
the quiet street an empty sleeve, darkness
like a pocket, I watch the circus come to town,
horses and elephants unloading to the hushed
commands of voices behind cigarettes,
hooves that sound empty clattering on the asphalt.
And a man trying to fix a broken hitch
kicks the metal casing, swears into a fist.
He looks away, and then looks toward me.

We believed this apartment would save us
by pushing us to either end of its three
terrific rooms, give us some space.
Your view was of shade collapsing the street,
our neighbor's fence; mine a linden's gray branches
that angled off like broken wings and dragged
across the roof next door. I am certain
this moment, two thousand miles west of me,
you are sleeping, just as I am certain
you write the history of our life together,
in letters to your friends.
The circus will be small: two elephants,

four horses, a trapezist. In the far dirt lot
a solitary figure arranges tent poles, sinks the heavy
stakes to their eyelets. Just below me the man
lights a cigarette and turns to his friend
who with two hands and a rope
is ready to raise the big top, who is calling
for help. It is beginning to be light, the tent
flaps along the ground like a disreputable flag.
My neighbor's gate is unlatched.
I can hear it creak, then slap back on itself.

Versions of Transport

The times you kept nothing to yourself
a slow turning was enough. The globe spun quietly
in the den. You hosed the failing pansies
while the child next door chased his shadow
with a stick. Winter passed on the island

like a single, full June, and there were friends
at any hour to drive away the sea birds, to bring
casseroles and wine. You understood then

that to see the future with clarity
was to stare into a fist. To invent
the honest stories engendered love
that was pitiable. Relax, you would say.

Breathe. What mattered was the full completion
of duty at the end of a row of roses,
the double portrait of sky on a calm, empty harbor,
though between days there was little to do,

sails drifting to black on an evening sea. Still,
the inner chorus was hopeful, like a pleasant forecast
with the curtains drawn. And wasn't it odd
how weather, stripped of freight, still denied
you an easy sleep, slow commitments
slowly blown, how the alimony of a story

was where you woke up, whether with
birds or without, in clothes or alone.
You sat so many mornings with a towel
around your shoulders and another on your lap,

discussing daylight with a friend who handled
daylight like a gun, who finally didn't make it.
You can see his face now and then, sketched
in angel dust and murmur. You can see it this second

as the sun starts to climb and the houses fill
with motion. Because you sit here in his honor.

And the rain this quiet morning will wash away
a lot of things, cocaine and old salt.
The substantial remains of terror.

Somewhere Someone is Saying Goodbye

I no longer pray for my brother,
who, out of work and bored, lazing in the tall grass
near the river, high and a little careless,
stubbed his cigarette in his best friend's hand,
who assured him it was fine, okay, and then, later,
beat him repeatedly with an empty mug.

I no longer pray for Catherine,
who came straight from the diner each morning
to sleep with her hands beneath my chin,
a week of moments in each curled fist, hands reminding me
of food, of the fear of being left alone at a counter,
daylight just beginning in the city's highest corners,
knowing it will be hours until the sun strikes
the pavement outside, until it is pleasant and safe
to walk to someone's home, and sleep.

I pray instead to a memory I have invented
to fill an empty room, a room like a chimney,
floor of ash, the roof a patch of sky
far over head. There is a song being sung nearby,
and though it sounds like Sarah it can't be,
for I have forgotten her in prayer
and simply phone when I'm in trouble.
There is someone saying goodbye over and over,
like the sound of rain rising at the window.
And in the rain is a fire.
And in the fire is my father, his hands
on his face and holding, I imagine, the first
tears he has ever felt. He stands so still
I expect him to vanish, like afternoon light
in a church by the river,

dissolving by degrees
into shadow and dust.

I finish my prayer with a list of sorrows:
be kind to Lynne, be gentle with Blake, laugh
with Grandfather, give Frank a sandwich.
The room is empty again
except for shoes and a few feathers, a foolish moonlight.
Somewhere, someone is saying goodbye.
The chimney cranes call across the rooftops.
They carry their burden home.

Peter Case

*I want to know more than I really
want to know,* and I should start
by asking the next table if they
could tell me something about
the woman I'm sitting with.
She's gone to the bathroom
and forgotten to lift away
her napkin first, so there it is
on the floor—a good way
of saying hello when I lean out
of my chair to pick it up,
but I don't. I mean I pick up
her napkin but the way they look
at me, I just sit back quietly.
So what have I done today?
Well, I woke up at a friend's
and felt alive for
the first time in weeks.
We just sat around for hours talking
in that frantic sign language
of old friends trying to reconnect.
Till now I'm here with this woman
who seems to know the whole club
and my friend talking to the bartender.
The ceiling is black
and strung with clear Christmas lights
so that four or five beers will
lower the sky and who knows how I'll
feel dancing so close to heaven.
The woman returns and looks at me
like I would a bowl of soup. Then says,
Have you heard this guy's music?
Thankfully, here's my friend with
a new drink and a smile, so I just nod.
I really don't know who we're here to see,

the marquee outside was a mystery
of past and future appearances.
He walks out in a suit my father
might've worn when he sold insurance
and his glasses are the kind
from Sears that make you look like
Buddy Holly or a scientist.
He says, My name is Peter Case,
and starts to strum a Rickenbacker
older than his suit.
In the stage lights his hat looks dusty,
then I see it really is, and he taps
a brown wing-tip and closes
his eyes, waiting for the words to arrive.
Then the world shuts down and my beer
goes warm, the stars come out
and I'm driving near Albuquerque
with the top down, and Peter Case
is with me. The desert spreads out
around us like a fallen summer sky
and the radio won't work so we're
singing a song about Satellite Beach.
There are lizards running from our
headlights like dancers on ether
and the cactus are pointing at God.
I lean back and watch
the constellations move to new places.
Peter Case is playing guitar,
steering with his knees, and we drive
through the night from song to song
never really noticing if where
we're going is getting any closer.

for A.J.

The Sea with Snow

When I am old I hope
to remember sadness unequivocally,
for somehow I will feel
less tired with my memories
if the lost and lied to
occupy with me that last, slender room.
It will be too late
for very much more
than nods to apparitions,
the silent friends who long ago
dismissed regret with the knowledge
that eternity is a long time.

Once, I grabbed my brother's wrist
as he reached from a higher branch,
as he whispered, "Okay now, hang on."
I saw myself in his eyes and felt
that to be truly helpless was a bit more
than this, the loose air
around me and leaves, like my hands today,
trembling beneath the pressure
of seconds passing.

Since then a few faces
have turned for good
toward the earth, though I know
I'm not alone.
Somewhere my brother lives quietly
with his hand around a glass,
and with words that are as good
as speech, except quieter.
And now and then each woman I've loved
is reminded of me,
though usually by the rain
or in a bar, a man's hand gone quiet

beside her own, the room filled
with lazy excuses to remain.

And what better than to remain
in a moment free of memory.
To ask the stranger
next to you if now seems the right time
to admit you've lied to him.
That you're not really here for company
or for solace,
or for love if it comes to that.
You'd just like to know if now is the right time,
as if it ever could be.
Since what we're waiting for
is the waiting.

Isabelle's Sister

I'm glad I met you. I'm happy
with the way we remind each other
of each other.
I have this habit of turning my back
on the one person in a room
willing to point out
that I'm out of control, that my shirt
looks like an ashtray. And there are lines
around my eyes like cracks leading out
from where two comets have struck the earth.
This is a lured confession,
and I want very much to keep from
erasing what little I like about myself.
At dawn, on Sundays, listening
to rain in the live oaks,
like an overheard promise whispered
sharply to a child, a child raised
on sharp promises,— I lose
the little weight I have in the world.
So that soon
the whole half-mast of things
becomes too evident to ignore, how everyone
starts out fine, a complete person,
then trembles to pieces as the window
is rolled up on a reasonable discussion,
the albums divided, files burned
and left to muddy the wet carpet
(wet with tears I might add, though that
is overstating things a bit). The days
wear on, crumbling the porcelain figurines
on the patio, forgotten in the settlement, until
we're too stunned to notice no one cares
if we've failed once or twice, no one
wants to witness our gray conclusion.
And you, who I'm so glad I've met, you

just want to be my friend, I realize that now.
Though maybe you'll love me, share your breakfast
when you're less hungry than you thought.
We can invent names for our different moods
(I'll be a paper cactus when sullen, you
a blue Sherpa when unappreciated).
But there it is again: hope. Never letting
well enough alone. Never admitting how
difficult it is, this business of failing
and going on.

Breakfast on the Patio

Despite the weatherman, who in hibiscus
and a grass skirt waved this morning
at a map of clouds, Jeff pulls on a pair
of sunglasses to watch the people walk by.
What he really wants is to go sailing,
which is okay with me, but the harbor
is smooth as an oil slick and breathless.
We watch a parade of moms and carriages,
the babies cooing the sunshine,
and a line of cyclists all tanned to
oblivion. Jeff goes for more coffee,

the boy next door walks by wearing
chaps and plastic six shooters.
I wave at his mother who is hosing down
the walk, and she waves back. Then I say, Bang
to the little guy but he just looks at me.
So I say, Hi, and he just looks at me.
Jeff returns with another plate of toast.
He still wants to sail but I raise a wet finger
and he nods like, Maybe later, then shakes out
the newspaper. Another cyclist pedals by
going, I guess, 20 miles an hour; I watch
the hanging fuchsia stir a bit in the sudden
wind. The phone rings and I look over at Jeff
but he's reading so I think, Oh well, and get up
to answer it. At the door I stop because
Jeff has asked, "You know what?" and I'm waiting
for whatever what is. "It doesn't get much better,"
he says, and we laugh. Phone still ringing

I go inside; the tape clicks on across the room,
I hear myself telling someone I'm not home,
then I hear someone say, "You're never home,
the problem with you is you're never home."

It's Kay, who I decide to call back later
but she goes on. "The problem with you is
you're never home when you're home.
You're not there when I look at you.
You don't say a thing when you say something."
Kay is on a roll but I go over
and pick up the phone. I'm home, I say
and I hang up. Then I go outside and look
at the smooth water, so smooth it seems fake.
"Who was it?" Jeff asks, still reading the paper.
The Harbor Queen is chugging past, a crowd
of tourists waves at me from its deck.
I lift my hand and say, It was for you.

Fear of Angels

So I think I'll stop, so tired of mumbling and
walking, slow collisions of dust and lung and those
other things arriving out of air like a sneeze,
how everyone needs help now and then.

But not now.
Downtown, in the easy
mingle of trash cans and the insane,
there's a fear of angels that pack
the missions, that hover
in the sleepy corners of an eye.

And whoever lives in a paper tent
folds with it and falls,
a mean vision of comfort
in the sway of city traffic.
I think to ignore myself long enough
is to remove every bandage.
And like Claude Rains
I have a list of bruises
and of kisses, a favorite table away from the noise.

But when I sit with coffee and retrieve
daylight from some other hour
I'm like everyone else

bearing the weight of a fragrant length of sky.
And were it easy to rise and touch the window
I'd count cars nudging home, the remarkable faces
waiting for soup.

Days before Grace

I am trying to be someone you can't see
without faith and a good heart,
mumbling toward an understanding with the earth,
the rain lately shaken from trees.

In place of effort my sister stitches hats
from yarn and sea glass,
and in place of love
I buy them at church bazaars
from ladies with Advent lavender for hair
and smiles that explain the impossible completions.
"Oh well," one says. "If not a hat
then a muffler for the phone."

One day and then the next.
And soon faucets are arrested, the river
locked in place and a street
so commonly flooded has given up its features.
The story begins, "I would never knowingly
break a heart," and ends
on page 37 of the June '88 issue;
I pick it up again and again, like the photo
of my family in San Diego, circa 1966,
father in Bermudas and mother
staring out of frame, my hand in my brother's.

Last night beside the river I turned
in your arms like an empty dress on a hanger.
What little moonlight left
fell to earth in pieces
and improved the river's loneliness,
like a table set with silver improves
the seldom used room. The wind's language
was less casual than speech,
and from the opposite bank a voice

chose its words from the Dictionary of Angels.
But we didn't listen.
Nearly always there's an echo
when the sun sets, as dusk's imprecision
is perfected by the night
and the earth does its best to sigh.
It was the only sound that could convince me
to hear the moon in the river,
the wind warming its hands in the sharp light
of stars, a voice describing hope to a man turning
in the arms of a ghost.

Explaining the Evening News to Corbyn

after Ben Watt

I heard Caruso last night for the first time, I'm 28.
My stepfather sat me in a lounge chair
the color of rain on new grass,
and said, "Listen, just listen." And I did.
Every time I express a fondness
he leaves an album out, a cassette tape by my car keys,
and with Caruso (like Rachmaninoff) it worked,
though I couldn't help saying the obvious,
how similar he seemed to Darby Crash.
One day you're eighteen in a freshman dorm,
gold and brown empties of Old English 800
crushed like metal cigarettes on the carpet—
The Lost Pilot is shaking in your hands.
Then it's Cavafy in a bathtub with
cinnamon candles welding themselves to the tiles
and the sprinklers outside interpreting rain.
Did I decide then never to have a child?

When I was sixteen I had never kissed a girl,
which is all you think about, aside from driving.
I would've nuzzled a broken bottle to hold Francesca's hand,
but what we said to each other
out of fear of saying anything
wasn't good for very much,
though it was better than whispering darkness
into a cup of clear water.
It wasn't true.

Corbyn lies in my arms now like the Prince of San Francisco.
His father, my oldest friend, laughs at me
from across the room because I can't keep
his baby's head from wobbling.
When I was Corbyn's age I had more hair
I think, and I might've been skinnier.

Kennedy was making plans
to bring Frost from Vermont
for the inauguration,
and life for my parents was as lyrical
as a cafeteria breakfast.
My sister will marry in a week
a man I've known and played tennis with
for twenty years. They sit with me now,
admiring Corbyn and thinking of names for a child
they are planning.
My sister has her hair tied back
like a Romanian gymnast, and when she looks at Corbyn
she smiles and is as beautiful as he is.
What I like about the evening news
is you can talk through it without missing anything,
which is what we're doing. But something's happened somewhere, so we
suddenly go quiet, as if an angel
in feathers has walked into the room.
I say, Corbyn, you're very lucky you can't hear any of this.
And then, like always, his head begins to wobble.
His mom reaches out to take him, and she kisses my cheek
in the same movement, so I feel relieved and scared
all at once, which is familiar enough to keep quiet about.
Corbyn's father walks toward the refrigerator
for a Coors and the dog puts his nose on my shoe.
It's a slow second and we wish
for a lot of things, the five of us,
for Corbyn to be okay forever
and for the child my sister hopes to have.
I suggest they call him Caruso, and we laugh.
What we really want, my sister says, is a little girl,
a little girl to marry Corbyn. Everyone's smiling.
An angel enters the room and it is clear:
we've got it all wrong.

Stories

Two girls, sisters I read, were witness to
the daily comings and goings of traffic
over a certain Central American road.
It's the kind of story you read about all the time,
a jungle as green as dollars, speckled
with tropical reds and yellows,

and birds everywhere, cawing or billowing up
toward, yes, a glazy blue sky.
These girls, sisters, set up a juice stand
by the road. And for weeks
soldiers and people traveling from one town
to the next stopped to have a drink

or just sit and wipe away a little dust, talk.
It got to be nothing unusual, two girls selling juice.
Then the soldiers, naturally, started dying.
No fever or sickness, just death. Fast
as falling rain. No one could figure it.
More weeks passed and nothing changed.

The conscripted farmers started rumors
about what these soldiers dreamt just before death;
the usual stuff, phantoms and jungle saints,
people seeing faces in the bark of trees;
you know how it goes. But it was the juice.
I guess you figured that by now.

The sisters probably loved, in the way of such stories,
a pair of brothers, guerillas from deep back
in the jungle. They were doing their part, these girls—
felt they had to probably, love and all;
you hear about these things. They didn't poison
by accident a passing priest or an uncle, and

we're not sure if something went wrong. But it's what
made you see Jesus today, I'm certain.
There's a field backing up to our house
and a road that goes I don't know how far, where trucks
drag their freight like small explosions;
it's a lousy road. And you were out there

in the rain most of the day thinking, like rain
will make a person do; you just gave in to that story.
Neither of us could kill a thing with less
than six legs; I know it, you know it;
it's what we said over breakfast.
But it's been raining for days, nights so loud

and insistent, we think it must be more than thunder,
more than any noise we've known. We're tired of it.
I'd like for you to come back in now.
It's entirely different at night, the way
we occupy our fears; and though there's hope in darkness,
we have no way of making sure. Come in and let me hold you.

There's no one else here, and I'm sure tomorrow
you'll be seeing again things that are really there.

The Hole in the Moon

I'm walking home wishing I was someone else,
and it's Sunday on the beach so everywhere I look
there are possibilities.
The moon's been funny this week, anchovies
are running the surf. People wade in
with nets and wire baskets, one boy
carries a cardboard box, but everybody
walks off with bait to sell or salt away.
Waves throw fish against the sand
and the shimmering is awful, the beach littered
for miles with little twitches of light.

Last night I was walking home
and stopped to watch some men string lights
from their car batteries to play basketball.
I hooked my fingers in the chainlink
and stood there while they shot around
then started playing.
But I was thinking about the Korean families
down for the day fishing, and the little girl
I'd seen earlier tugging a sandshark toward a bucket.
So when one guy dropped the ball
and swung at his friend, I went home

and slept, woke-up and went to breakfast
at RUBY'S-On-the-Pier. Now these anchovies
all over the beach, kids screaming
or their parents screaming.

It's not like I hate it, but I do.
On a Wednesday in March
I sat here with you, not a sandwich
in sight. The air was quiet and clear,
and Catalina seemed close enough to touch,
like we could walk to it. I bet today

we could, on the backs of all these fish;
if you were here I think we'd try.
So I sit and wish for that, and for this tide
to drop. I guess, really, I'm wishing for something less,
a hole in the moon maybe, and from it
a small pill of hope. But I don't say anything.
I just close my eyes like I always did,
like someone who's trying to remember,
and place you nearby
where, by chance, I might be going.

Notes

These poems take their titles from the following: "Reasons to Live" from the book of the same title by Amy Hempel; "Grace to Be Born and Live" from the poem "In Memory of My Feelings" by Frank O'Hara (the phrase also serves as his epitaph); "When You Wish upon a Star that Turns into a Plane" from the song "Valentine" by The Replacements; "So Long Lonely Avenue" from the song by Rickie Lee Jones; "See How We Are" from the song by John Doe and Exene Cervenka; "Everywhere at Once" from the song by Peter Case; "Moods for Moderns" from the song by Elvis Costello.

Recent Carnegie Mellon Titles

1982
The Granary, Kim R. Stafford
Calling the Dead, C.G. Hanzlicek
Dreams Before Sleep, T. Alan Broughton
Sorting It Out, Anne S. Perlman
Love Is Not a Consolation; It Is a Light, Primus St. John

1983
The Going Under of the Evening Land, Mekeel McBride
Museum, Rita Dove
Air and Salt, Eve Shelnutt
Nightseasons, Peter Cooley

1984
Falling from Stardom, Jonathan Holden
Miracle Mile, Ed Ochester
Girlfriends and Wives, Robert Wallace
Earthly Purposes, Jay Meek
Not Dancing, Stephen Dunn
The Man in the Middle, Gregory Djanikian
A Heart Out of This World, David James
All You Have in Common, Dara Wier

1985
Smoke from the Fires, Michael Dennis Browne
Full of Lust and Good Usage, Stephen Dunn (2nd edition)
Far and Away, Mark Jarman
Anniversary of the Air, Michael Waters
To the House Ghost, Paula Rankin
Midwinter Transport, Anne Bromley

1986
Seals in the Inner Harbor, Brendan Galvin
Thomas and Beulah, Rita Dove
Further Adventures With You, C.D. Wright
Fifteen to Infinity, Ruth Fainlight
False Statements, Jim Hall
When There Are No Secrets, C.G. Hanzlicek

1987
Some Gangster Pain, Gillian Conoley
Other Children, Lawrence Raab
Internal Geography, Richard Harteis
The Van Gogh Notebook, Peter Cooley
A Circus of Needs, Stephen Dunn (2nd edition)
Ruined Cities, Vern Rutsala
Places and Stories, Kim R. Stafford

1988
Preparing to Be Happy, T. Alan Broughton
Red Letter Days, Mekeel McBride
The Abandoned Country, Thomas Rabbitt
The Book of Knowledge, Dara Wier
Changing the Name to Ochester, Ed Ochester
Weaving the Sheets, Judith Root

1989
Recital in a Private Home, Eve Shelnutt
A Walled Garden, Michael Cuddihy
The Age of Krypton, Carol J. Pierman
Land That Wasn't Ours, David Keller
Stations, Jay Meek
The Common Summer: New and Selected Poems, Robert Wallace
The Burden Lifters, Michael Waters
Falling Deeply into America, Gregory Djanikian
Entry in an Unknown Hand, Franz Wright

1990
Why the River Disappears, Marcia Southwick
Staying Up For Love, Leslie Adrienne Miller
Dreamer, Primus St. John
Two Long Poems, Gerald Stern

1991
Permanent Change, John Skoyles
Clackamas, Gary Gildner
Tall Stranger, Gillian Conoley
The Gathering of My Name, Cornelius Eady
A Dog in the Lifeboat, Joyce Peseroff
Raised Underground, Renate Wood
Divorce: A Romance, Paula Rankin